Bootstrap:
The ultimate beginners guide to Bootstrap 3.0

Table Of Contents

Introduction

One of the most common problems that you can encounter while designing your own website or creating your own application is the lack of uniformity when it comes to the construction of these aspects. This is especially difficult when you are using the conventional method of programming because this requires you to pay very close attention to a lot of mundane details. In fact, even a minor error can make all of your enormous efforts go to waste.

Because this is one of the most common problems that you can encounter on a regular basis, it is perfectly understandable for you to look for a specific tool that can help you address this concern. By doing so, you can definitely save a lot of time, effort, and resources in the process. This is where the Bootstrap 3 framework comes into the picture.

Fortunately, this book has been designed to help orient you to Bootstrap. By knowing the fundamentals of Bootstrap 3 framework, you will have an easier time making the necessary coding for your website and creating unique layouts for your applications.

Bootstrap is considered as a set of tools that can help you design your website or software using uniform methods, source codes, and other aspects of designing that you need to make interesting aspects for application and site use.

This book contains some of the fundamental facts that you need to know about Bootstrap 3 framework. Also, you will be oriented to the process of programming, designing, and other important components of the tool set. Along with these facts are some tips and other pointers in designing using the Bootstrap 3 framework.

There are numerous benefits that you can obtain from reading this book and understanding the concepts that come with this:

- You will learn to appreciate the significance of the tool set in programming and designing through added knowledge regarding Bootstrap 3 framework.

- It will be easier to design and program web pages and applications by determining the fundamentals of the tools under the compilation.

Aside from these benefits, you can surely gain more skills that you can share to developers and other people who want to contribute to the already existing pool of knowledge and source codes, among other facts about designing and programming that you have to learn. This will make it easier for you to create your own sets of techniques and modify the already existing ones.

Chapter 1: Introduction to Bootstrap

A Bootstrap is a program that can help you initialize the OS (operating system) during the startup phase. This may also refer to the entire process of starting up your computer or device. This pertains to the activation of small and loading programs while each of the programs is connected to the next application that should be executed in sequence.

Bootstrap is a free collection of web based and browser based tools for creating web applications and web pages.

Developers typically incorporate templates. These templates will make it easier to insert certain elements that you want to see in your site or application. The interface components include the following:

- Optimal JavaScript extensions

- Navigation

- Buttons

- Forms

- Typography

The ultimate goal of this tool set is to develop the interface that can bring consistency across various internal tools.

Bootstrap may also refer to the incremental preparation of early programming environments.

In the long run, this can help you create user friendly and more complex programming environments. For instance, if your programming environment consists of a simple text editor and an assembler program, you can come up with gradual improvements on these things. In the long run, these changes can lead to the object oriented and sophisticated programming of the current graphical IDEs (integrated development environments).

There are various features that Bootstrap 3 framework can boast of.

This is a type of tool set that can dynamically adjust. This is particularly true for mobile devices because most of the features that you can find in this tool set are especially designed for these devices. Therefore, if your mobile device has an older browser, Bootstrap can downgrade for this particular browser so you can still view it without much difficulty. Also, this is compatible with the latest versions of all types of major browsers.

This framework is also open source. Therefore, numerous developers and other specialists can contribute to the already existing pool of source codes and commands that you can readily use for designing. Because this is an open source framework, developers are highly encouraged to:

- participate in the project the best way that they can

- make their own major or minor contributions to this platform

- adapt the Bootstrap file. By doing so, they can select the particular components that they wish to incorporate for their personal projects

There are numerous intricacies when it comes to the structure and function of this platform.

Bootstrap 3 framework is considered as a modular compilation. This is composed of a series of stylesheets for LESS that can help you in successfully implementing the different components that comprise the tool kit. You can make your adjustments through a stylesheet with central configuration system. Using the LESS declarations will help you notice profound changes in the system. As for the LESS style language, you can have a good chance of using the following:

- mix ins

- nested selectors

- functions and operations

- variables

In the documentation, you can use the customization option. You may choose from the desired components. Also, the system can readily adjust the values of different options to the specific needs if necessary.

Aside from the components mentioned above, the platform can offer responsive design and the grid system or the variable width layout (as the alternative). These can help provide numerous variations of resolutions and kinds of devices that may be used. Some of the devices and components that may be used are the following:

- personal computer units and tablets with high and low resolutions

- landscape and portrait orientation

- variations of different types of devices and resolutions

The CSS stylesheet can provide you with fundamental style definitions for your site or application.

This can help you achieve a modern and uniform appearance for formatting the following:

- form elements

- tables

- text

Aside from these, this stylesheet has reusable components that contain other types of interface elements that you can readily use.

This also has buttons with some advanced button features such as progress bar, warning messages, thumbnails, advanced typographic capabilities, labels, pagination, breadcrumb navigation, navigation, vertical and horizontal tabs, navigation and make lists, and drop down option.

During the process of start up, various diagnostic tests will be performed.

One of these includes the POST (power on self test). This is the process of checking or setting configurations for the device. This can also help implement the routine testing for peripheral connection, external memory devices, and hardware. The program is then loaded so it can readily initialize the operating system.

Some of the programs that can help load the operating system are the following:

- NIC or network interface controller utilizes a type of bootloader that can support booting from a certain network interface like PXE (pre-boot execution environment) or Etherboot.

- LILO or Linux loader is a type of Linux bootloader that typically runs from a floppy disk or a hard drive.

- NTLDR or NT loader is the bootloader intended for Windows NT operating system of Microsoft. This normally runs from your hard drive.

- GRUB or GNU grand unified bootloader is a kind of multiboot specification that permits you to select one of different kinds of operating systems.

The JavaScript components can provide you with additional user interface elements like carousels, tool tips, and dialog boxes.

Also, these can help extend the function of most types of existing interface elements in your system.

- The Dojo Bootstrap can help implement the main Bootstrap system using the Dojo tool kit.

- On the other hand, the UI Bootstrap can provide controls for the Angular JS. This port can help you reuse some of the Bootstrap mark up concerns.

There are numerous uses of Bootstrap 3 framework that you can definitely depend on.

First, this can help you download the Bootstrap CSS stylesheet. This can also include a link within the HTML file. As for the JavaScript components, you can use this as a reference along with your jQuery library.

Chapter 2: Tools for Bootstrap

The entire process of web designing usually requires you to acquire numerous skills and learn different disciplines. This is the case when it comes to the maintenance and creation of websites and applications. These particular areas of web designing include graphic or web designing, interface designing, authoring, search engine optimization, experience designing, standardized code creation, and proprietary software creation. For this book section, you will learn more about some of the tools that you can use along with Bootstrap. In the long run, this will make it easier for you to design various sites.

Easel is considered as a very impressive tool that you can use for browser designing.

This is a tool that can help you create specific elements in the documents link to the other documents. In turn, this can aid in making specific changes to the prototype flows in your software within using a line of code. You may even have the users test a unique link that will allow you to obtain feedback in the earlier part of the process. This tool can help highlight the part of the design that you are currently interested in. After this, you may simply include your comment.

Bootsnipp is regarded as an element gallery for the web designs and the web developers.

You may use this tool to help you design elements and code snippets. These will eventually be used for Bootstrap JS, CSS, or HTML framework. This tool has a mailing list that you have to subscribe to so you can obtain application updates in the future.

Bootstrap Designer is a type of online designing tool that can help you come up with excellent HTML5 templates that are heavily based on Bootstrap framework.

You have to use to Bootstrap designer to help you make numerous designs like clean and creative, monochromatic look, typographic driven, grunge, black and white, and minimalist style.

Fancyboot is considered a simple but powerful customization tool used for Bootstrap.

This contains the optimal amount of control for its interface. At the same time, this does not include all of the unnecessary complexities in a tool.

Paintstrap is another Bootstrap tool that can help you construct unique themes by using the COLOURlovers or Adbor kuler color schemes.

For the first part of the customization, you need to input your desired color scheme. To do this, you have to input the permalink URL or the theme ID of the color scheme that you wish to apply. Next, you should set the specific colors that you will use for the website or the application. Finally, you have to download the required CSS files.

The Bootstrap Button Generator is regarded as one of the simplest ways to help you come up with new button styles.

The generated buttons are highly compatible with the Bootstrap 3 framework. To use this tool, you need to enter the CSS class that you want to assign to the new button styles. After this, you may try out the other button colors. This will help you update the live previews on the right side of the tool. As soon as you are ready, you just have to copy the code along the bottom part then add this to the page found below bootstrap.min.css. This will enable you to use the button of your choice.

Font Awesome allows you to come up with iconic font styles that are especially designed for Bootstrap.

This can provide you with scalable vector icons. You can instantly customize these vector icons to make your site or application more interesting. This tool can help you manipulate elements like drop shadow, color, and size.

GetkickStrap is a tool that seamlessly mixes the top tier web technologies along with Bootstrap.

This is so advanced that this can help you run a database driven and authenticated web application. This is possible without having a native backend. Partner of Kickstrap with JSPM.io can provide a strong type of package dependency front end manager that is built on Require.js. Kickstrap applications are regarded as JSPM bundles with static resources. These can be operated any time in the lifetime of the web application.

Bootstrap Magic is a theme generator that typically features Angular JS and the Bootstrap 3 framework.

You can easily come up with your very own Bootstrap theme quickly. Also, you can instantly see what you are currently changing at the content. You may also add in some awesome web fonts derived from Google Webfont. These are all included in the font magic typehead. To maximize using this application, you may download the personalized CSS, minified variables, standard variables, and LESS variables.

DivShot can be as simple as your mock up tool.

However, this can also be as powerful as the text editor that you may have used in the past. This tool is considered a representative of a fast and visual front end development. DivShot is considered as a type of drag and drop editor that permits you to come up with responsive sites on Foundation as well as Bootstrap. Through this tool, this is possible without the bothersome coding.

Bootply is an application that allows you to fiddle with Bootstrap.

Using this tool, you can readily edit Bootstrap friendly JavaScript, HTML, and CSS. You may use this to quickly build and design interfaces. This is possible by utilizing the drag and drop editor intended for Bootstrap. This features leverage for code repository. Using this tool can help you grab Bootstrap templates, examples, and snippets.

You may use this tool to help you test, extend, prototype, and design the Bootstrap framework. This is integrated along with other types of Bootstrap plugins, frameworks, and micro-libraries.

The Grid Displayer is a type of in browser web designer.

This can help display the grid of your preferred front end framework. Unfortunately, this is not available for mobile devices. This tool is a bookmarklet that can help display both fixed and fluid kinds of grids. This works well with WebKit and Firefox browsers.

Jetstrap is considered not just as a type of mock up tool but also as a premier interface constructing tool for Bootstrap 3 framework.

This is especially made for idea people, designers, and developers. Jetstrap can help you create awesome websites with fast running connections without using up too much effort to dig through your documents.

X-editable permits you to construct editable elements for your page.

This may be utilized with any type of engine like jQuery, jQuery-ui, and Bootstrap. This tool can support in place editing using pure jQuery, jQuery UI, or Bootstrap. Moreover, the tool includes both inline and popup modes. Some editable elements that you can create on your page through this library include inline and popup modes. This is considered as the new life of Bootstrap editable plugins that the developers can still improve and refactor in the long run.

This can support different input types like checklist, dateui, date, select, textarea, and text. Furthermore, this can support server side and client side validation. You can fully customize the container placement as well. Users can toggle manually, through double clicking or clicking. This works in all the modern browsers like IE7+.

Layoutit can help you construct the front end code quickly and simply with Bootstrap.

This is possible by utilizing the drag and drop interface constructor. The tool takes every component and element of Bootstrap so you can make the front end coding much easier without having to be a specialist in CSS 3, HTML 5, or

JavaScript. All of your designs may be Fluid and Responsive CSS. This is easy to integrate with just about any type of programming language. All you have to do is to just download the HTML and start off coding your design in it.

Chapter 3: Getting Started with Bootstrap

One of the most common concerns related to Bootstrap is how to get started. In this book section, you will learn some of the fundamental pieces of information on how you can begin using this platform for designing.

In getting started with the Bootstrap 3 framework, you need to download the files from the platform first.

These are different types that you may want to check out before you decide to download one of them. These appeal to various skill levels and use cases. You may then manage and install Bootstrap's fonts, JavaScript, CSS, and LESS using Bower. To install this, you have to use this command: $ bower install bootstrap.

- Bootstrap has the fonts, JavaScript, compiled CSS, and minified CSS. There are no original source files or doc files included.

- Source code requires some setup and a LESS compiler. Along with the documents are the font files, JavaScript, and source LESS.

- Bootstrap CDN is a type of support designed for JavaScript and CSS. You just have to use the following CDN links:

  - For the latest minified and compiled JavaScript, you may try out this string:

    ```
    <script
    src="//maxcdn.bootstrapcdn.com/bootstrap/3.2.0/js/bootstrap.min.js"></script>
    ```

  - For optional themes, you may want to input the following:
    ```
    <link rel="stylesheet"
    href="//maxcdn.bootstrapcdn.com/bootstrap/3.2.0/css/bootstrap-theme.min.css">
    ```
  - As for the latest minified and compiled CSS, this should do the trick:
    ```
    <link rel="stylesheet"
    href="//maxcdn.bootstrapcdn.com/bootstrap/3.2.0/css/bootstrap.min.css">
    ```
- SASS is a type of Bootstrap derivative ported from the LESS to SASS for easier inclusion of Compass, Rails, and SASS only projects.

Bootstrap is downloadable in two main forms where you can find various files and directories. In turn, these can help logically group the resources and provide both the minified and compiled variations. You have to take note that jQuery is required. This is typically shown in the starter template. You may consult your bower.json to help you see the jQuery versions that are supported in your system. These are the things that you can download from the official platform:

- Clicking on the "Download Bootstrap" button can help you download the minified and precompiled versions of fonts, JavaScript, and Bootstrap CSS. There are no original source code files or documentation included.

- On the other hand, clicking on the "Download Source" button can help you obtain the latest updated Bootstrap JavaScript and LESS source codes directly from GitHub.

If you work using the uncompiled source code of Bootstrap, you may have to compile the LESS files. This will help you produce CSS files that you can readily use. If you want to compile LESS in CSS, you should take note that Bootstrap only officially supports Recess.

You may then deal with the precompiled Bootstrap as soon as you have finished downloading.

You may then unzip the compressed folder. Unzipping this can help you clearly see the main structure of your compiled Bootstrap. This form is considered as the fundamental form. You may use the precompiled files for fast drop in usage for just about any web project that you may have at the moment. The developers can provide you with compiled CSS as well as JS (bootstrap. *). Also, this can provide you with minified and compiled JS and CSS (bootstrap.min. *). Fonts from Glyphicons are usually included because this is regarded as the optional theme for your Bootstrap.

The Bootstrap source code downloads include documentations, JavaScript, Source LESS, font assets, and precompiled CSS.

This includes the following source codes:

- less/

- js/

- fonts/

- dist/

  o css/

  o js/

  o fonts/

- docs-assets/

- examples/

- *.html

The fonts/, js/, and less/ are considered as the source codes for the font icons,, JavaScript, and CSS, respectively. On the other hand, the dist/ folder most likely includes everything that has been listed within the precompiled download section. The docs/ folder has the source code for the documentation. Finally, the examples/, docs-assets/, and *html/ show some samples of Bootstrap usage. Beyond these source codes, the rest of the included files provides support for development, license information, and packages.

A fundamental HTML template that uses Bootstrap typically includes bootstrap.min.css, bootstrap.min.js, and jquery.js files.

These files are used to help create a typical HTM file for Bootstrapped Template. The basic template will more or less look like this:

<!DOCTYPE html>

<html>

  <head>

    <title> The Bootstrap Template </title>

    <meta name="viewport" content="width=device-width, initial-scale=1">

    <! – Bootstrap -->

    <link href="css/bootstrap.min.css" rel="stylesheet">

    <!—HTML5 Shim and Respond,js IE8 support of HTML5 elements and media queries -->

    <!—WARNING: Respond.js doesn't work if you view the page via file:// -->

  <!—[if lt IE 9]>

    <script src="https://oss.maxcdn.com/libs/html5shiv/3.7.0/html5shiv.js"> </script>

    <script src="https://oss.maxcdn.com/libs/respond.js/1.3.0/respond.min.js"> </script>

  <![endif]-->

  </head>

  <body>

    <h1> Insert Content Here </h1>

```
<!-- jQuery (necessary for Bootstrap's JavaScript plugins) -->

<script src="https://code.jquery.com/jquery.js"> </script>

<!—Include all compiled plugins (below), or include individual as needed -->

<script src="js/bootstrap.min.js"> </script>

</body>

</html>
```

Bootstrap utilizes Grunt for the build system.

This contains convenient methods that can help you work using the framework. Through Grunt, you can readily, test run and compile your codes.

To help you install Grunt, you should initially download and install node.js.

This includes npm (node packaged modules). This is a way to help you manage the development dependencies through node.js. After downloading and installing, you need to look for the following from the command line:

- Globally install the grunt-cli with npm install –g grunt-cli.

- Navigate to root /bootstrap/ directory. After this, run the npm install command. The npm will check out the package.json file and will automatically install the required local dependencies that are listed there.

Once you have completed these steps, you can run the different Grunt commands that are provided from the command line itself.

The following are the available Grunt commands:

- grunt

  This can help you run tests and build absolutely everything. Also, this command can help you minify and compile JavaScript and CSS, regenerate the Customizer assets, run the HTML 5 validator against your documents, build your documentation website, and so much more. If you are currently hacking on Bootstrap itself, you will not need this.

- grunt test

  The command can heedlessly run QUnit and JSHint tests in PhantomJS.

- grunt watch

  Whenever you save a change, this command can help watch your LESS source files so the system can automatically recompile them to CSS.

- grunt dist

This can simply help you compile JavaScript and CSS. Also, this can assists in regenerating the /dist/ directory using minified and compile JavaScript and CSS files. This is typically the command that you will be looking for.

You may also need to perform some troubleshooting for the system once in a while.

If you encounter problems in running Grunt commands or installing dependencies, you have to delete the /node_modules/ directory that has been generated through npm. You may then have to rerun the npm install command.

Chapter 4: CSS and Its Intricacies

The cascading stylesheets, also known as CSS, is considered as a form of style sheet language typically utilized to help you describe the appearance and the formatting of a certain document that has been written using a markup language. You will need this for user interfaces and to written in XHTML and HTML. This may also be applied to the Bootstrap 3 framework.

You need to keep some facts in mind when you want to use the CSS functions in the Bootstrap 3 framework for your endeavors.

To help you get started with the Bootstrap 3 framework, you need to download the file first. After this, you should unzip the archive file. Because there are too many files that you can find within your downloaded package, you have to sort out the folders and the files that you do not need to help you with constructing your site or your application.

After this, you need to directly jump to the dist directory and copy all of the folders into another destination. This is considered as your project home. For your project, you need to take care of three directories. Under these directories, there exist four types of CSS files. These are the following:

- The bootstrap.css is considered as your main CSS file. This should be included in all of your HTML pages.

- On the other hand, bootstrap.min.css is the minified version of bootstrap.css. This can help your application online.

- The bootstrap-theme.css is regarded as an additional CSS file. This is an optional file that you can store in your project compilation. This can provide you with three dimensional effects on some elements of your project like the buttons.

- Finally, bootstrap-theme.min.css is the minified version of your CSS file.

Once you have established the folders and files that you will need for your page or application, you have to create the JS folder. This should include the following files:

- bootstrap.js

- bootstrap.min.js

These files contain the main JavaScript libraries for Bootstrap. This can provide libraries for powerful JavaScript functionalities like the following:

- search auto suggest

- drop down menus

- carousels

There are various advantages of using the font files instead of some flat images in designing your web page or application.

First, this can consume less bandwidth than your typical web pages. Therefore, this can help in speeding up your website connection. Aside from this, the font icons are all resizable and responsive. These font icons are also known as glyphicons.

Using the key pieces of the Bootstrap 3 infrastructure, you can have a better chance of having a stronger, faster, and better approach to web development.

HTML 5 doctype is a requirement for Bootstrap 3 framework so it can help you utilize various CSS properties and certain HTML elements. Bootstrap 3 framework utilizes certain CSS properties and HTML elements that usually require using the HTML 5 doctype. You have to include this at the beginning of most of the projects that you plan to implement in the future:

```
<!DOCTYPE html>

<html lang="en">

...

</html>
```

This should be implemented if you want to have the English language as the primary communication language for the final project. You may use this alternative code in the beginning of your projects:

```
<!DOCTYPE html>

<html>

...

</html>
```

During the Bootstrap 2 framework days, you will notice certain optional friendly styles for certain key aspects of this framework.

However, with the latest framework (Bootstrap 3), the project has been rewritten to promote a more mobile friendly environment from the start. Instead of having the need to add on some of the optional mobile styles, they have already been created right in the core. In fact, you will see that this platform is a "mobile first" framework. In accordance with this claim, you will find numerous mobile first styles in the entire library instead of finding them inside numerous separate files. To help ensure that you will have proper touch zooming and rendering, you need to add the viewport meta tag to the <head> by inserting the following command:

```
<meta name="viewport" content="width=device-width, initial-scale=1">
```

Alternatively, you may use this code:

```
<meta name="viewport" content="width=device-width, initial-scale=1.0">
```

Take note of the following aspects:

- The initial-scale=1.0 or initial-scale=1 will make sure that when these are loaded, the web page will eventually be rendered in a 1:1 scale. Also, there will be no zooming applied outside the box.

- On the other hand, the width property will help you control the display width for the targeted device. Setting this to device-width can help ensure that this will be rendered across numerous devices like tablets, desktops, and mobile phones properly.

You may disable the zooming capability in your mobile device.

You may do this by adding the command *user-scalable = no* to your viewport meta tag. This will help disable the zooming function readily. This means that you will only be able to scroll through the pages where this command has been implemented. This will make the results in the web page seem more of a native application. Overall, this is not recommended for every site. Therefore, you have to practice caution in implementing this:

```
<meta name="viewport" content="width=device-width, initial-scale=1, maximum-scale=1, user-scalable=no">
```

Bootstrap can also help set the basic global link styles, typography, and basic global display for your system.

Specifically, the developers can help you execute some helpful commands.

Take note that these styles will be found in scaffolding.less.

- Setting your global link color through @link-color then apply the link underlines only on your :hover can help improve the link styles.

- As for typography, you may utilize the @line-height-base, @font-size-base, and @font-family-base attributes as your typographic base

- For the basic global display, you may set the background-color: #fff; as part of the site or application <body> element.

If you want to utilize LESS code, you may locate these in scaffolding.less.

To help you attain an improved rendering for cross browsing purposes, you have to utilize normalize.css. This is a project spearheaded by Jonathan Neal and Nicolas Gallagher.

You will also need containers or containing elements to help you wrap the site contents and eventually house your grid system.

For starters, you may be interested to select at least one of the two containers that will be used in the projects.

- You may utilize .container the help you obtain a responsive type of fixed width container.

  div class="container">

  ...

  </div>

- If you want to have a full width container, you may use .container-fluid. This will help span the viewport's entire width.

  <div class="container-fluid">

  ...

  </div>

- In the bootstrap.css file, you will see the .container class:

  .container {

    margin-left: auto;

    margin-right: auto;

    padding-left: 15px;

    padding-right: 15px;

- You have to take note that because of factors such as padding, you will notice that both of the containers are not nestable. Check out this bootstrap.css file:

  @media (min-width: 768px) {

    .container {

      width: 750px;

    }

You will notice that the CSS has media-queries for the containers with width. This can help in applying responsiveness for your project. Also, this can help you modify the container class accordingly. In the long run, this can help you in properly rendering the grid system.

The Bootstrap 3 framework can also permit you to create responsive images.

You may do this by incorporating a class .img-responsive to your <img> tag. This class can apply height: auto; and max-width: 100%; to the images. In the long run, this can help the image scale nicely in relation to its parent element.

<img src="..." class="img-responsive" alt="Responsive image">

The platform can help you use Normalize so you can establish consistency when it comes to cross browser concerns.

Normalize.css is considered an HTML 5 ready and modern alternative to the CSS resets. This is a relatively small CSS file that can help provide you with a more efficient and more effective cross browser consistency in the default style of the HTML elements.

Chapter 5: The Grid System

The Bootstrap 3 platform also utilizes a mobile first and responsive fluid grid system that can scale up to 12 columns as the viewport size or device viewing size increases. This also includes predetermined classes that can help you easily lay out your options. This will also help you incorporate powerful mix-ins so you can generate more semantic layouts.

There are numerous ways that you can define a grid.

In the field of graphic designing, the grid is typically regarded as a form of two-dimensional structure. This is composed of a set of intersecting horizontal and vertical lines utilized to help construct content for your web page or application. This is widely utilized to design content and layout structure in print designing.

As for web designing, this is considered as an effective procedure that can help you come up with a consistent layout. You may effectively and rapidly do this using CSS and HTML. To put this simply, the grids that you use in web designing can help you structure and organize content, reduce the cognitive load on site visitors, and make your websites easier to scan.

The Bootstrap grid system is a mobile first and responsive scheme that can appropriately scale up to 12 columns.

Scaling takes place as the viewport size and device size increase. This typically includes numerous predefined classes that can provide you with easy options for layouting. Also included are the powerful mix-ins that can help you come up with more semantic layouts.

The Bootstrap 3 framework is considered as a mobile first platform in the sense that the codes that are used for Bootstrap currently start off by targeting the smaller screens of tablets and other types of mobile devices. For larger screens of desktops and laptops, the grids and other components are the "expanded".

The mobile first strategy employed for the Bootstrap grid system consists of some important components.

First, the content can help you identify the most important factors that you have to consider. On the other hand, the layout is aimed to cater to the smaller widths first. The progressive enhancement will help you add some elements as the size of your screen increases.

The grid system is typically utilized to help you come up with page layouts by virtue of a series of columns and rows.

In turn, these columns and rows can help in housing your content. The following can somehow explain how this system can work for you:

- The rows should be placed in a .container-fluid or a .container to help attain proper padding and alignment. The former is used to achieve full width effects while the latter is used for fixed widths.

- You should use rows to help you create a horizontal group of columns.

- You have to place the content in columns. On the other hand, the columns may be considered as immediate derivatives of the rows.

- Some of the predetermined grid classes like .col-xs-4 and .row may be considered as immediate derivatives of the rows. To help you achieve more semantic layouts, you may incorporate fewer mix ins.

- Columns can create gutters through various padding functions. Gutters are the gaps that you can find in between the column contents. The padding will be offset in series of rows for the first and the last columns through the negative margin on .rows.

- The negative margin is the main factor that makes the rest of the factors in CSS outdented. This makes the contents in the grid columns lined up with lots of grid contents.

- You can come up with grid columns by indicating the specific number of twelve sets of available columns that you want to span. For instance, you can end up with four equal columns by using four .col-xs-4.

- If you place more than twelve columns in a single row, each of the group of excess columns will wrap in a new line as a unit.

- The classes of grids may apply to certain device that contain screen widths that are more than or equal the breakpoint sizes. These should override the grid classes that are targeted at smaller devices. Therefore, implementing any type of .col-md- class to any type of element can not only impact the style on medium sized devices but also affect the overall style of the large devices. This is so if there is no .col-lg- class present.

As for grid options, you can see how different aspects of Bootstrap grid system can work across numerous devices using a handy table.

Utilizing a set of .col-md-* grid classes can help you come up with a fundamental grid system that will start out stacked on the tablet and the mobile devices or the extra small up to the small range. This takes place before it turns horizontal for the desktop or the medium sized devices. You may place the grid columns in any .row.

The following are aspects of the Bootstrap grid system and how these can work across various devices. Take note that all of these are nestable. There are also offsets for all devices. As for column ordering, this is also applicable for all devices.

- Extra small devices
  - Grid behavior is horizontal all of the time.
  - There is no maximum container width. This is set at automatic for these devices.
  - Class prefix is .col-xs-
  - There are 12 columns.
  - Maximum column width is also set at automatic.
  - Gutter width is 30 px. There are 15 px for each side of the column.
- Small devices
  - Grid behavior is initially collapsed. This is horizontal above breakpoints.
  - Maximum container width is 750 px.
  - Class prefix is .col-sm-
  - There are 12 columns.
  - Maximum column width is 60 px.
  - Gutter width is 30 px. There are 15 px for each side of the column.
- Medium devices
  - Grid behavior is initially collapsed. This is horizontal above breakpoints.
  - Maximum container width is 970 px.
  - Class prefix is .col-md-
  - There are 12 columns.
  - Maximum column width is 78 px.
  - Gutter width is 30 px. There are 15 px for each side of the column.
- Large devices
  - Grid behavior is initially collapsed. This is horizontal above breakpoints.
  - Maximum container width is 1170 px.
  - Class prefix is .col-lg-

○ There are 12 columns.

○ Maximum column width is 95 px.

○ Gutter width is 30 px. There are 15 px for each side of the column.

This is the fundamental structure of the Bootstrap grid:

<div class="container">

  <div class="row">

   <div class="col-*-*"> </div>

   <div class="col-*-*"> </div>

  </div>

  <div class="col-*-*"> </div> ... </div>

</div>

<div class="container"> ....

With the four divisions of grids that are readily available to you, you are eventually bound to encounter issues where the columns will not clear quite correctly because one of them is apparently taller than the other.

To help you address the issue, you have to utilize a certain combination of the responsive utility classes and a .clearfix. Aside from clearing columns at certain responsive breakpoints, resorting to resetting pulls, pushes, or offsets may also help you in the long run.

Offsets are regarded as a helpful feature that can help you have more specialized layouts.

This can help you adjust the columns by using them to push these columns. By doing so, you can have more spacing for your text and other types of contents. The .col-xs=* classes do not readily support offsets. However, you can easily replicate them by utilizing an empty cell.

You may move the columns towards the right by using the .col-md-offset-* classes. These can help you increase the left margin of your column by a specific number of * columns. The * symbol stands for a specific value that you want to implement. For instance, if you want to move .col.sm-4 over five columns, you need to use .col-sm-offset-5. You can enter a value that can range from 1 to 11.

The nested rows should have a set of columns.

In turn, these columns can pile up to 12 or less. You are not required to use all of the 12 available columns. To help you nest the content along with the default grid, you have to incorporate a set of .col-sm-* and add in a new .row in an already existing .col-sm-* column.

Using the column ordering feature can help you easily write the columns in a certain given order and then show them somewhere else.

Column ordering can help you in easily changing the order of the built in grid columns with .col-sm-pull* and col-sm-push-* modifying classes.

This is an example of the main structure for column ordering:

<div class="row">

    <div class="col-sm-8 col-sm-push-2"> .col-sm-8 col-sm-push-2 </div>

    <div class="col-sm-2 col-sm-pull-8"> .col-sm-2 col-sm-pull-8 </div>

</div>

In addition to the prebuilt grid classes intended to achieve fast layouts, the platform includes mix ins and LESS variables to help generate your very own semantic and simple layouts quickly.

The following are some of the aspects that fall under the LESS variables and mix ins:

- You may modify the variables using example usage to help you attain your own customized values. Also, you may also use mix ins with the given default values. To help you use the default settings to come up with a two column layout with a gap in between, you have to enter the following:

  .wrapper {

      .make-row();

  }

  .content-main {

      .make-md-column(8);

  }

  .content-secondary {

      .make-md-column(3);

      .make-md-column-offset(1);

  }

  <div class="wrapper">

```
<div class="content-main"> ... </div>

<div class="content-secondary"> ... </div>
```

</div>

- Mix ins are typically used along with the grid variables. This will help you generate semantic CSS that you can use for individual grid columns. You have to place the following codes to incorporate this feature in your web page or your application:

  - Generation of large column offsets

```
.make-lg-column-offset(@columns) {

  @media (min-width @screen-lg-min) {

    Margin-left: percentage((@columns / @grid columns));

  }

}

.make-lg-column-push(@columns) {

  @media (min-width @screen-lg-min) {

    left: percentage((@columns / @grid columns));

  }

}

.make-lg-column-pull(@columns) {

  @media (min-width @screen-lg-min) {

    right: percentage((@columns / @grid columns));

  }

}
```

  - Generation of large columns

```
.make-lg-column(@columns; @gutter: @grid-gutter-width) {

  position: relative;
```

    - Prevent the columns from collapsing when they are empty

      min-height: 1 px;

    - Inner gutter through padding

```
            padding-right: (@gutter / 2);

            padding-left: (@gutter / 2);

        ▪ Width calculation based on the number of available columns

            @media (min-width: @screen-lg-min) {

              float: left;

              width: percentage((columns / @grid-columns));

              }

            }
```

o   Creation of medium column offsets

```
    .make-md-column-offset(@columns) {

      @media (min-width @screen-md-min) {

        Margin-left: percentage((@columns / @grid columns));

      }

    }

    .make-md-column-push(@columns) {

      @media (min-width @screen-md-min) {

        left: percentage((@columns / @grid columns));

      }

    }

    .make-md-column-pull(@columns) {

      @media (min-width @screen-md-min) {

        right: percentage((@columns / @grid columns));

      }

    }
```

o   Creation of medium columns

```
    .make-md-column(@columns; @gutter: @grid-gutter-width) {

      position: relative;
```

- Prevent the columns from collapsing when they are empty

  min-height: 1 px;
- Inner gutter through padding

  padding-right: (@gutter / 2);

  padding-left: (@gutter / 2);
- Width calculation based on the number of available columns

  @media (min-width: @screen-md-min) {

  float: left;

  width: percentage((columns / @grid-columns));

  }

  }

o Generation of small column offsets

.make-sm-column-offset(@columns) {

@media (min-width @screen-sm-min) {

Margin-left: percentage((@columns / @grid columns));

}

}

.make-sm-column-push(@columns) {

@media (min-width @screen-sm-min) {

left: percentage((@columns / @grid columns));

}

}

.make-sm-column-pull(@columns) {

@media (min-width @screen-sm-min) {

right: percentage((@columns / @grid columns));

}

}

- Generation of small columns

  .make-sm-column(@columns; @gutter: @grid-gutter-width) {

  position: relative;

  - Prevent the columns from collapsing when they are empty

    min-height: 1 px;

  - Inner gutter through padding

    padding-right: (@gutter / 2);

    padding-left: (@gutter / 2);

  - Width calculation based on the number of available columns

    @media (min-width: @screen-sm-min) {

    float: left;

    width: percentage((columns / @grid-columns));

    }

  }

- Generation of extra small columns

  .make-xs-column(@columns; @gutter: @grid-gutter-width) {

  position: relative;

  - Prevent the columns from collapsing when they are empty

    min-height: 1 px;

  - Inner gutter through padding

    padding-right: (@gutter / 2);

    padding-left: (@gutter / 2);

  - Width calculation based on the number of available columns

    @media (min-width: @grid-float-breakpoint) {

    float: left;

    width: percentage((columns / @grid-columns));

    }

```
        }
```

- Creation of wrapper for a specific series of columns

  .make-row(@gutter: grid-gutter-width) {

  - Clearing the floated columns

    .clearfix();

    @media (min-width: @screen-md-min) {

    margin-right: (@gutter / -2);

    margin-left: (@gutter / -2);

    }

  - Negative margin rested rows out for alignment of the contents of columns

    .row {

    margin-right: (@gutter / -2);

    margin-left: (@gutter / -2);

    }

- Variables can help you determine the gutter width, the specific number of columns, and the media query point where the floating columns should start off. These are mainly used to help generate the semantic CSS. In turn, this is used for individual grid columns. These are used to help generate predefined grid class and customized mix ins. These are some examples of codes that you can incorporate in your project:

  @grid-float-breakpoint: 768px;

  @grid-gutter-width: 30px;

  @grid-columns: 12;

You have to utilize the media queries to help you come up with some of the key breakpoints for your grid system.

Media query is also known as the conditional CSS rule. This can help you simply apply some CSS along with your source codes based on specific conditions that have been set forth before the actual insertion of the conditions. If you have met these conditions, the style will then be applied. You can readily find the media queries in the LESS files.

In Bootstrap 3 framework, media queries permit you to hide, show, and move content based on the size of your viewport. To help you create some key breakpoints in the grid system, you have to use these for your LESS files. The following are some of the media queries that you may use in LESS files:

- For extra small devices like phones with less than 768 px, you have to use no media query because this is considered as the default in Bootstrap.

- For small devices like tablets and other devices with 768 px and up: @media (min-width: @screen-sm-min) { ... }

- For medium devices like desktops with 992 px and up: @media (min-width: @screen-md-min) { ... }

- For large devices like large desktops with 1200 px and up: @media (min-width: @screen-lg-min) { ... }

You have to expand these so you can include a max-width. This will help you limit the CSS to narrow down the set of devices that you will target. You may execute these by doing the following:

- Extra small devices: @media (max-width: @screen-sm-max) { ... }

- Small devices: @media (min-width: @screen-sm-min) and (max-width: @screen-sm-max) { ... }

- Medium devices: @media (min-width: @screen-md-min) and (max-width: @screen-md-max) { ... }

- Large devices: @media (min-width: @screen-sm-min) { ... }

The media queries have two main parts. These are the size rule and the device specification. Regardless of the type of min-width: @screen-sm-min, if the screen width gets smaller than the @screen-sm-max, you have to do something about it. This applies to all types of devices where you plan to implement your codes.

Chapter 6: The Art of Typography

Basically, typography refers to the technique and the art of arranging type so you can make recognition of language most appealing to those who will view this.

The art of typography requires you to select the appropriate elements that can draw in your site visitors toward your web pages. Some of these elements include the following:

- Kerning or the adjustment of the spaces between the pairs of letters

- Tracking or the adjustment of spaces between certain groups of letters

- Leading or line spacing

- Line length

- Point size

- Typefaces

Typography can help create a unique experience for the users even before they have clicked a button or read a word from your web page or application. This can also provide the "personality" of your website. This is very important because this can contribute to the overall response of your visitors to your website.

There are numerous sections of typography in Bootstrap that you have to know.

Bootstrap can utilize Sans-serif, Arial, Helvetica, and Helvetica Neue as its default font stacks. By using Bootstrap's typography feature, you can readily create inline elements like lists, paragraphs, and headings.

- All of the HTML headings from <h1> to <h6> are available. They are all styled in Bootstrap. This is important when you want to closely match the font style of your heading but still prefer the text to be shown inline. You may create inline subheading with a secondary lighter text in any type of heading using the .small class or a generic <small> tag.

- As for the lead body copy, you may add the class="lead". This will help you add some interesting emphasis to a certain paragraph. This will also yield a font with taller line height, lighter weight, and larger size.

- For body copy, the global default size of Bootstrap is 14 px with line height of 1.428. You may apply this to the <body>. Also, you may implement this for all of your paragraphs. Additionally, <p> or paragraphs can help receive a bottom margin of around 50 percent of the computer line height. The default is set at 10 px.

- In variables.less, there are LESS variables where the typographic scale is heavily based on. These are the @line-height-base and @font-size-base. The @font-size-base refers to the bas base font size that will be used for the entire script. On the other hand, the @line-height-base helps you adjust the height of the base line. You have to use these variables and some simple logic to help you come up with your preferred line heights, paddings, and margins. You may customize these things at Bootstrap adapts.

- For emphasis, you have to use tags like <strong> and <em>. These are considered as default tags.

  o The <em> tag. helps emphasize text that are set in Italics

  o On the other hand, the <strong> tag is mainly used for text that has relatively heavier font weight.

- The inline elements are aspects of HTML that are typically contrasted with the block level elements. These can take up the content width. There are various elements that are under this category:

  o Marked text is a helpful function of inline elements if you want to highlight a certain run of text because of the text's relevance in another context. For this function, you simply have to insert the <mark> tag.

  o To help you indicate deleted blocks of text, use the <del> tag.

  o To insert strikethrough text, use the <s> tag.

  o If you want to indicate certain additions that you made for a certain document, you need to use the <ins> tag.

  o To help you de-emphasize blocks of text or inline text, you have to use the <small> tag. This will help reduce the size of the text at around 85 percent of the size of the parent text. The heading elements typically receive their individual font sized for the nested <small> elements. Alternately, you may utilize an inline element containing the .small place as a substitute for the <small> tag.

  o Using the <b> tag can help you emphasize a certain snippet of text using heavier font weight.

  o On the other hand, utilizing the <i> tag can help emphasize text using italics.

  o Underlined text warrants the use of the <u> tag.

- To help you change text in components, you have to use text capitalization classes. These may also be referred to as the transformation classes.

  <p class="text-capitalize"> Capitalized text. </p>

  <p class="text-uppercase"> Uppercased text. </p>

  <p class="text-lowercase"> Lowercased text. </p>

- For easier text realignment to components, you may use text alignment classes.

  <p class="text-left"> Aligned to the left. </p>

  <p class="text-right"> Aligned to the right. </p>

  <p class="text-nowrap"> Text with no wrap. </p>

  <p class="text-justify"> Justified text. </p>

  <p class="text-center"> Aligned to the center. </p>

- The HTML element can provide you with markup for acronyms or abbreviations like HTTP and WWW.

  - For basic abbreviation, the stylized implementation of the <abbr> element for acronyms and abbreviations help show expanded version on hover. The elements with this tag will appear along with a light dotted border. You can find this at the bottom. You may view the full text on hover as long as you will incorporate the content to the <abbr> title attribute.

    <abbr title="attribute"> attributed </abbr>

  - If you want to go for a slightly small font size, you have to add .initialism to the abbreviation that you want to target.

    <abbr title="Cascading Style Sheets" class="initialism"> CSS </abbr>

- Using the <address> tag can help you readily display the contact information on the web page. This tag can help you show contact information of the entire body of work or its nearest counterpart. Because the <address> tag typically reverts to display:block; you need to utilize certain tags to help you insert line breaks to your enclosed address text. You may preserve the formatting by ending all of your lines using the <br> tag.

- If you want to incorporate content and style changes for the simple variations, you need to insert the conventional <blockquote> tag. You may use this around any of your HTML text.

  - Alternately, you may insert a <small> tag to help you identify the main source of your quote.

  - Also, you may set align the blockquote to the right using the .pull-right class. You may also use the .blockquote-reverse class for this.

    <blockquote class="blockquote-reverse">

    Insert content here.

    </blockquote>

  - For straight quotes, you may use the <p> tag.

    <blockquote>

      <p> Insert quote here.

    </p>

    </blockquote>

  - To help you name a certain source, you need to insert the <footer> tag to help you identify the source easily.

    <blockquote>

      <p> Insert quote here.

    </p>

      <footer> A person famous in <cite title="A Certain Source"> A Certain Source </cite> </footer>

    </blockquote>

  - You may then wrap the name of your source work in <cite> tags.

Bootstrap can also support definition lists, unordered lists, and ordered lists.

Along with the lists, there are various list elements that will be discussed in this section.

You may also use inline for your lists.

You should place all of the list items in a single line using display: inline-block; and some of the light padding.

```
<ul class="list-inline">
  <li> ... </li>
<ul>
```

For the unstyled lists, you have to get rid of the default list style and the left margin on the list items.

This may apply for only the immediate children. This means that you have to add the class for any type of nested lists as well.

```
<ul class="list-unstyled">
  <li> ... </li>
</ul>
```

The unordered lists are referred to as the lists that do not have any kind of specific order.

This is conventionally styled using bullets. If you do not wish to see the bullets, you may then get rid of the styling using the .list-unstyled class. You may also insert all your list items in a single line by using the .list-inline class.

```
<ul>
  <li> ... </li>
</ul>
```

The ordered list is a list of items where the order explicitly matters.

In other words, the items in the list fall in a certain sequential order. Because of this, the order is typically prefaced using numbers.

```
<ol>
  <li> ... </li>
</ol>
```

The items in the definition lists are composed of both the <dd> and the <dt> elements. This can help you come up with a list of terms along with the associated descriptions. The <dt> stands for the definition term. Like the trusty dictionary, the words that you will insert in between tags will be the phrase or the terminology that you intend to define. Subsequently, the <dd> tag is just the definition for the <dt>.

```
<dl>
  <dt> ... </dt>
```

<dd> ... </dd>

</dl>

You may make the descriptions and terms in the <dl> tag line up side by side if you use the class dl-horizontal. This typically starts off stacked like the default <dl> tags. However, when the navigation bar expands, so do these.

<dl class="dl-horizontal">

<dt> ... </dt>

<dd> ... </dd>

</dl>

The horizontal description lists typically truncate terms that are too lengthy to fit on the left column. This is done by inserting text-overflow. In the narrower viewports, these will change to your default stacked layout.

The Bootstrap 3 framework permits you to utilize display codes using two different key methods.

These are the main ways that you can resort to:

- If you are planning to display your codes inline, you have to insert the <code> tag.

  For this example, the <code>&lt;code&gt;</code> should be wrapped as an inline.

- Another method that you may use is the <pre> tag. If you have to display your codes as a form of standalone block element, you have to use this tag. This is also applicable for code with multiple lines. You have to make sure that you will escape any of the angle brackets that you can find in the code to help promote proper rendering.

  <pre>&lt;p&gt;Place your sample text here. &lt;/p&gt;</pre>

  You may optionally include the .pre-scrollable class. This will help set the maximum height of 350 px. Also, this can help provide the y-axis scrollbar for your web page.

- For variables, you need to include the <var> tag.

  <var> y </var> = <var> x </var> + <var> z </var>

To help you indicate blocks sample output from a certain program, you need to insert the <samp> tag.

Chapter 7: Tables and Bootstrap

Tables can help you organize not only a certain group of text but also relevant images and media that come with the contents. In this book section, you will learn more about tables and how you can incorporate them in your web pages using various styles.

Bootstrap can provide you with a clean layout for constructing tables.

These are certain table elements that Bootstrap supports:

- The <table> tag is considered as a wrapping element that can help you display items in a tabular format. If you want basic styling, this should be your tag of choice. This will provide your text with only horizontal dividers and some light padding. You may swap the tag for the .table class.

  <table class="table">

  Insert contents here.

  </table>

- The <caption> tag provides the summary or the description of what a certain table holds.

- On the other hand, the <th> tag inserts a special form of table cell for the row or column. This will highly depend on the placement and the scope labels. This should always be used in a <thead> tag.

- A <td> tag is used for default table cells.

- The <tr> tag serves as a container element for a certain set of table cells. In most cases, these table cells are the <th> and the <td> tags. These cells appear in a single row.

- You may use the <tbody> tag as a container element for the table rows or the <tr> in the body of your table.

- The <thead> tag is used as a container element for the table header rows or the <tr> so you can label the table columns accordingly.

Aside from the .table class and the base table markup, there are other additional classes that you may utilize to help you style the markup.

This section will provide you with a glimpse of all the classes.

- To help you achieve a condensed table, you need to add the .table-condensed class. This will cut the row padding in half. This is done to help make the tables more compact. This is especially helpful if you prefer denser information.

```
<table class="table table-condensed">
```

Insert contents here.

```
</table>
```

- Hover tables can be incorporated in your web page if you add the .table-hover class. After inserting this class, a background with light gray hue will be added to the rows when you hover the cursor over them. You have to add the class to help enable the hover state on the table rows found within a <tbody> tag.

```
<tableclass="table table-hover">
```

Insert contents here.

```
</table>
```

- You will obtain borders that can surround every element when you add the .table-bordered class. This will also help incorporate rounded corners for the entire table.

```
<table class="table table-bordered">
```

Insert text here.

```
</table>
```

- If you want to incorporate some stripes on the rows within the <tbody> tag, you need to insert the .table-striped class. The stripes are also referred to as the zebra stripes.

  For this class, you need to consider your cross browser compatibility. Keep in mind that striped rows and tables in general are styled using the :nth-child CSS selector. This selector is currently not available for the Internet Explorer 8 browser.

```
<table class="table table-striped">
```

Insert contents here.

```
</table>
```

The contextual classes will permit you to modify the background color of the individual cells or the background shade of the table rows.

You may apply these classes to <th>, <td>, or <tr>.

- The .danger class indicates a potentially negative or dangerous action.
- On the other hand, the .success class may indicate a positive or successful action.

- You may use the .warning class to denote a warning that requires some or a lot of attention.

- The .active class applies your chosen hoven color to a specific cell or row.

As for the responsive tables, you can make the table horizontally scroll up for the small devices that are under 768 px.

You may do this by wrapping any .table class within a .table-responsive class. When you view the table on a device with a width that exceeds 768 px, you will not notice any difference in the tables.

<div class="table-responsive">

 <table class="table">

 Insert content here.

 </table>

</div>

Firefox browser has some of the awkward styling that involves the width command. This typically interferes with most responsive tables.

@-moz-document url-prefix() {

 Fieldset { display: table-cell; }

}

This set of codes is used to override this concern.

Chapter 8: Forms: The Basics

Online forms are considered as really important aspects for your web pages because this can help promote the rate of interaction between you and the site visitors. Specifically, the site visitors can use these as their medium of expressing themselves when they have the need to do so. These are also typically used if you want to provide access to sites for a limited number of people who will visit the page regularly. In this book section, you will learn the fundamentals of incorporating online forms for your web page.

There are various form layouts that you have to know and learn.

To date, there are three main types of form layouts. These are the following:

- The horizontal form stands out from the other two types not only because of the amount of markups that it possesses but also because of the presentation of the forms. To help you come up with a form that utilize this type of layout, you have to perform the following:

    o Add a .control-label class to your labels.

    o Wrap the control and the labels in a <div> using the .form-group class.

    o Add the .form-horizontal class to its parent <form element>

If you want to add take note that if you add the .form-horizontal class to your form, there will be no need to add .row class because the .form-group classes will behave as the grid rows.

<form class="form-horizontal" role="form">

  <div class="form-group">

    <label for="inputEmail3" class="col-sm-2 control-label">Email</label>

    <div class="col-sm-10">

      <input type="email" class="form-control" id="inputEmail3" placeholder="Email">

    </div>

  </div>

  <div class="form-group">

    <label for="inputPassword3" class="col-sm-2 control-label">Password</label>

```html
<div class="col-sm-10">
    <input type="password" class="form-control" id="inputPassword3" placeholder="Password">
  </div>
</div>
<div class="form-group">
  <div class="col-sm-offset-2 col-sm-10">
    <div class="checkbox">
      <label>
        <input type="checkbox"> Remember me
      </label>
    </div>
  </div>
</div>
<div class="form-group">
  <div class="col-sm-offset-2 col-sm-10">
    <button type="submit" class="btn btn-default">Sign in</button>
  </div>
</div>
</form>
```

- The inline form functions can help you construct forms where all the elements are inline. The labels are alongside and the elements are all left aligned. You need to add the .form-inline class into your <form> tag.

```html
<form class="form-inline" role="form">
  <div class="form-group">
    <label class="sr-only" for="exampleInputEmail2">Email address</label>
    <input type="email" class="form-control" id="exampleInputEmail2" placeholder="Enter email">
```

```
          </div>
   <div class="form-group">
    <div class="input-group">
     <div class="input-group-addon">@</div>
     <input class="form-control" type="email" placeholder="Enter email">
    </div>
   </div>
   <div class="form-group">
    <label                                              class="sr-only"
for="exampleInputPassword2">Password</label>
    <input            type="password"            class="form-control"
id="exampleInputPassword2" placeholder="Password">
   </div>
   <div class="checkbox">
    <label>
     <input type="checkbox"> Remember me
    </label>
   </div>
   <button type="submit" class="btn btn-default">Sign in</button>
  </form>
```

This will only apply to the forms in viewports. The viewports should be at least 768 px wide. This also requires custom widths. Text areas, selects, and inputs are all 100 percent wide in Bootstrap by default. To utilize the inline form, you have to set the width in the form controls used within.

As much as possible, you have to add the appropriate labels for the forms. The site visitors will have some trouble with your online forms if you do not include labels for each input. For the inline forms, you may hide the labels by inserting the .sr-only class.

- The vertical or the basic form directly comes with the Bootstrap platform. The system can automatically control the individual forms to they can receive some simple but interesting global styling.

```
<form role="form">
```

```html
<div class="form-group">
  <label for="exampleInputEmail1">Email address</label>
  <input type="email" class="form-control" id="exampleInputEmail1" placeholder="Enter email">
</div>
<div class="form-group">
  <label for="exampleInputPassword1">Password</label>
  <input type="password" class="form-control" id="exampleInputPassword1" placeholder="Password">
</div>
<div class="form-group">
  <label for="exampleInputFile">File input</label>
  <input type="file" id="exampleInputFile">
  <p class="help-block">Example block-level help text here.</p>
</div>
<div class="checkbox">
  <label>
    <input type="checkbox"> Check me out
  </label>
</div>
<button type="submit" class="btn btn-default">Submit</button>
</form>
```

You have to do the following so you can come up with the basic form:

- Add the .form-control class for all of your textual <select>, <textarea>, and <input> elements.

- Wrap the controls and the labels within a <div> with the .form-group class. This is required for optimum spacing.

- Add the role form to your parent <form> element.

You should not directly combine the form groups with the input groups. Instead, you have to nest the input groups in the form group.

Bootstrap normally supports the most typical form controls.

They are also referred to as the supported form controls. Some of them include select, radio, checkbox, textarea, and input.

Inputs are considered as the most common form of text field.

This is where the users will be required to enter most of their vital form data. Bootstrap 3 framework can offer support for all of the native HTML5 input types like color, tel, search, url, email, number, week, time, month, date, datetime-local, datetime, password, and text. The proper type declaration is also needed to make theInputs fully styled for your web page needs. To help you add integrated buttons or text before and after the text based <input> tag, you have to assess the input group components first.

<input type="text" class="form-control" placeholder="Text input">

On the other hand, the text area is mainly used if you need to have numerous lines for input.

You may then change the attribute of the rows command as you deem fit. One of the adjustments that you can create is the modification of the number of rows. If you decide to make some adjustments in this area, you have to take note that more rows will yield larger boxes while fewer boxes will make you end up having smaller boxes.

<textarea class="form-control" rows="3"></textarea>

The radio buttons and the checkboxes are excellent if you want the site visitors to choose from a certain list of preset options.

If you will build a form, you have to use the checkbox command. This will help you if you intend the visitor to choose any number of choices from your list. On the other hand, you have to use the radio option to limit the amount of choices to only one selection.

- For the stacked or default radio, you have to take note that the disabled attribute should be appropriately style. To have to add the .disabled class to the <fieldset>, .checkbox-inline, .checkbox, .radio-inline, or .radio. This will make the <label> tag for the radio of checkbox display the "non-allowed" cursor everytime the site visitor hovers over the label involved.

  <div class="checkbox">

   <label>

    <input type="checkbox" value="">

```
    Option one is this and that&mdash;be sure to include why it's great
   </label>
 </div>
 <div class="checkbox disabled">
  <label>
   <input type="checkbox" value="" disabled>
   Option two is disabled
  </label>
 </div>


 <div class="radio">
  <label>
   <input type="radio" name="optionsRadios" id="optionsRadios1"
value="option1" checked>
   Option one is this and that&mdash;be sure to include why it's great
  </label>
 </div>
 <div class="radio">
  <label>
   <input type="radio" name="optionsRadios" id="optionsRadios2"
value="option2">
   Option two can be something else and selecting it will deselect option
one
  </label>
 </div>
 <div class="radio disabled">
  <label>
   <input type="radio" name="optionsRadios" id="optionsRadios3"
value="option3" disabled>
```

Option three is disabled

```
  </label>

</div>
```

- For the inline radios and checkboxes, you have to use the .radio-inline and the .checkbox-inline classes. You have to implement these on a series of radios or checkboxes for controls that will show up on the same line.

```
<label class="checkbox-inline">

  <input type="checkbox" id="inlineCheckbox1" value="option1"> 1

</label>

<label class="checkbox-inline">

  <input type="checkbox" id="inlineCheckbox2" value="option2"> 2

</label>

<label class="checkbox-inline">

  <input type="checkbox" id="inlineCheckbox3" value="option3"> 3

</label>


<label class="radio-inline">

  <input type="radio" name="inlineRadioOptions" id="inlineRadio1" value="option1"> 1

</label>

<label class="radio-inline">

  <input type="radio" name="inlineRadioOptions" id="inlineRadio2" value="option2"> 2

</label>

<label class="radio-inline">

  <input type="radio" name="inlineRadioOptions" id="inlineRadio3" value="option3"> 3

</label>
```

The select is typically used when you want to permit the site visitors to select from numerous options.

By default, this will only allow one choice. You have to use the <select> tag for the list options which the site visitors are familiar with. These may include numbers and states. If you want the site visitor to choose more than one option, you have to incorporate multiple="multiple".

```
<select class="form-control">

  <option>1</option>

  <option>2</option>

  <option>3</option>

  <option>4</option>

  <option>5</option>

</select>


<select multiple class="form-control">

  <option>1</option>

  <option>2</option>

  <option>3</option>

  <option>4</option>

  <option>5</option>

</select>
```

If you want to place plain text beside a form label, you may have to use static control.

The form label should be found in a horizontal form. Use the .form-control-static class in a <p> tag if you are aiming for this type of form layout.

```
<form class="form-horizontal" role="form">

  <div class="form-group">

    <label class="col-sm-2 control-label">Email</label>

    <div class="col-sm-10">

      <p class="form-control-static">email@example.com</p>

    </div>
```

```
</div>

 <div class="form-group">

  <label for="inputPassword" class="col-sm-2 control-label">Password</label>

  <div class="col-sm-10">

   <input    type="password"    class="form-control"    id="inputPassword"
placeholder="Password">

  </div>

 </div>

</form>
```

**Bootstrap 3 framework can offer extensive styling for the disabled
classes and inputs that are intended for form validation.**

The form control state can help make this possible for you.

*For input focus, you have to get rid of the default outline command styles for
some forms controls.*

In its place for :focus, you have to apply a box-shadow.

*If you have to disable a certain input, you have to simply add the disabled
attribute.*

This will not only disable it but also change the mouse cursor and the styling as
soon as your cursor hovers on the target element. You may include the disabled
Boolean attribute to an input. This will help prevent user from placing inputs on a
certain location and eventually end up with a slightly different look of the web
page.

```
<input        class="form-control"        id="disabledInput"        type="text"
placeholder="Disabled input here..." disabled>
```

*To disable all of the controls in the <fieldset> tag at once, you need to insert the
disabled attribute to a target <fieldset>.*

For disabled fieldsets, there exists a caveat especially regarding the functionality
of the <a> tag. The styles mentioned in this book section utilize the pointer-
events: none command. This is used in an attempt to disable the link
functionality for <a class="btn btn-*"> buttons. However, that specific CSS
quality is not yet standardized. Also, this is not yet fully support in browsers like
Opera 18 and Internet Explorer 11. If you want to play safe, you need to utilize
customized JavaScript to disable the involved links.

There are still cross browser compatibility issues for this certain function. While
Bootstrap 3 framework will definitely implement the styles for all types of

browsers, browsers like Internet Explorer 9 and below still cannot support the disabled attribute found on a <fieldset>. You have to use customized JavaScript to help you disable the fieldset for these browsers.

```
<form role="form">

 <fieldset disabled>

  <div class="form-group">

   <label for="disabledTextInput">Disabled input</label>

   <input type="text" id="disabledTextInput" class="form-control" placeholder="Disabled input">

  </div>

  <div class="form-group">

   <label for="disabledSelect">Disabled select menu</label>

   <select id="disabledSelect" class="form-control">

    <option>Disabled select</option>

   </select>

  </div>

  <div class="checkbox">

   <label>

    <input type="checkbox"> Can't check this

   </label>

  </div>

  <button type="submit" class="btn btn-primary">Submit</button>

 </fieldset>

</form>
```

You may insert the readonly Boolean attribute in your input.

This will help prevent user from styling and modifying the input as disabled.

```
<input class="form-control" type="text" placeholder="Readonly input here..." readonly>
```

The Bootstrap 3 framework incorporates validation styles for success states, warning, and error on form controls.

To use this, you need to add .has-success, .has-error, or .has-warning to the parent elements. Any .help-block, .form-control, and .control-label within that particular element will eventually receive the validation styles.

<div class="form-group has-success">

 <label class="control-label" for="inputSuccess1">Input with success</label>

 <input type="text" class="form-control" id="inputSuccess1">

</div>

<div class="form-group has-warning">

 <label class="control-label" for="inputWarning1">Input with warning</label>

 <input type="text" class="form-control" id="inputWarning1">

</div>

<div class="form-group has-error">

 <label class="control-label" for="inputError1">Input with error</label>

 <input type="text" class="form-control" id="inputError1">

</div>

With the help of .has-feedback combined with the right type of icon, you may also incorporate optional feedback icons.

Manual positioning of the feedback icons is needed for inputs without labels and for input groups coupled with an add-on to the right. You are highly encouraged to provide some labels for all of the inputs. This is deemed important for accessibility reasons. If you want to prevent the display of labels, you need to hide this using the sr-only class. If you have to do this without labels, you simply have to adjust the top value of your feedback icon. For the input groups, you simply have to adjust the right value to your desired pixel value. The value will depend on the specific width of your add on.

- This is the usual string of tags and classes for the optional icons:

  <div class="form-group has-success has-feedback">

  <label class="control-label" for="inputSuccess2">Input with success</label>

  <input type="text" class="form-control" id="inputSuccess2">

```html
<span class="glyphicon glyphicon-ok form-control-feedback"></span>
</div>
<div class="form-group has-warning has-feedback">
<label class="control-label" for="inputWarning2">Input with warning</label>
<input type="text" class="form-control" id="inputWarning2">
<span class="glyphicon glyphicon-warning-sign form-control-feedback"></span>
</div>
<div class="form-group has-error has-feedback">
<label class="control-label" for="inputError2">Input with error</label>
<input type="text" class="form-control" id="inputError2">
<span class="glyphicon glyphicon-remove form-control-feedback"></span>
</div>
```

- If you want to have optional icons in your inline and horizontal forms, you should use the following set of commands:

```html
<form class="form-horizontal" role="form">
<div class="form-group has-success has-feedback">
<label class="control-label col-sm-3" for="inputSuccess3">Input with success</label>
<div class="col-sm-9">
<input type="text" class="form-control" id="inputSuccess3">
<span class="glyphicon glyphicon-ok form-control-feedback"></span>
</div>
</div>
</form>
```

Alternatively, you may use this set of tags and classes:

```html
<form class="form-inline" role="form">
```

```
<div class="form-group has-success has-feedback">

    <label     class="control-label"     for="inputSuccess4">Input     with
success</label>

    <input type="text" class="form-control" id="inputSuccess4">

    <span class="glyphicon glyphicon-ok form-control-feedback"></span>

  </div>

</form>
```

- You need to incorporate the .sr.only class on your label for the form
controls that have no visible label. Bootstrap 3 framework will
automatically adjust the current position on your icon once this has been
added.

```
<div class="form-group has-success has-feedback">

    <label     class="control-label     sr-only"     for="inputSuccess5">Hidden
label</label>

    <input type="text" class="form-control" id="inputSuccess5">

    <span class="glyphicon glyphicon-ok form-control-feedback"></span>

  </div>
```

**Form control sizing allows you to set widths and heights of your
forms by using class.**

To help you adjust the form heights, you may use the .input-lg class. For the form
width, you have to use the .col-lg class.

- Using the height sizing feature can help you create shorter or taller forms
controls that help match the button sizes.

```
<input class="form-control input-lg" type="text" placeholder=".input-lg">

<input class="form-control" type="text" placeholder="Default input">

<input  class="form-control  input-sm"  type="text"  placeholder=".input-
sm">


<select class="form-control input-lg">...</select>

<select class="form-control">...</select>

<select class="form-control input-sm">...</select>
```

- You may quickly size the form controls and size labels in .form horizontal by incorporating .form-group-sm or .form-group-lg.

```
<form class="form-horizontal" role="form">

 <div class="form-group form-group-lg">

   <label                 class="col-sm-2                control-label"
for="formGroupInputLarge">Large label</label>

   <div class="col-sm-10">

     <input  class="form-control"  type="text"  id="formGroupInputLarge"
placeholder="Large input">

   </div>

 </div>

 <div class="form-group form-group-sm">

   <label                 class="col-sm-2                control-label"
for="formGroupInputSmall">Small label</label>

   <div class="col-sm-10">

     <input  class="form-control"  type="text"  id="formGroupInputSmall"
placeholder="Small input">

   </div>

 </div>

</form>
```

- For column sizing, you have to wrap the inputs in any custom parent element or grid columns. This will help enforce the desired widths easily.

```
<div class="row">

 <div class="col-xs-2">

   <input type="text" class="form-control" placeholder=".col-xs-2">

 </div>

 <div class="col-xs-3">

   <input type="text" class="form-control" placeholder=".col-xs-3">

 </div>

 <div class="col-xs-4">
```

```
<input type="text" class="form-control" placeholder=".col-xs-4">

    </div>

  </div>
```

Bootstrap 3 platform also has form controls that can help you have block help text.

This text flows along with the inputs. To help you insert a full width block for content, you need to incorporate the .help-block class after the <input> tag.

<span class="help-block">A block of help text that breaks onto a new line and may extend beyond one line.</span>Above is an example of block level help text intended for form controls.

Conclusion

Hopefully, this book has provided you with increased awareness about the Bootstrap 3 framework as well as some skills in programming and designing through knowledge on the tool set.

After learning the series of concepts for creating and designing applications and web pages, you have to implement what you have learned in this book. By applying what you have learned from this book, you will easily find your way in designing most types of applications and web pages without going through much difficulty in constructing and designing.

Thank you and good luck!